# HEAL THE SICK

Gospel Healing Teaching for the New Man

DAVID O'BRIEN

© 2019 by *David O'Brien*
ISBN: 978-0-9828843-8-6

All rights reserved. This book is protected by the copyright laws of the United States of America. This book may not be copied or reprinted for commercial gain or profit. The use of quotations or photocopying for personal or group study, or for free distribution without distorting the original work, is permitted and encouraged. Credit and contact information must be included as follows: "Heal The Sick," ActsChristianity.com, Copyright © 2019, Used by permission." Other permission may be granted upon request.

**Scripture quotations are taken from the following Bible versions:**

The New King James Version. Copyright © 1982 by Thomas Nelson, Inc. Used by permission. All rights reserved
The NEW AMERICAN STANDARD BIBLE®, Copyright © 1960,1962,1963,1968,1971,1972,1973,1975,1977, 1995 by The Lockman Foundation. Used by permission.
The Holy Bible, English Standard Version copyright © 2001, 2007, 2011, 2016 by Crossway Books and Bibles, a Publishing Ministry of Good News Publishers. Used by permission. All rights reserved.
King James Version (KJV), 1611, 1769. Outside of the United Kingdom, the KJV is in the public domain.

**Abbreviations are as follows:**
**NKJ** – New King James Version
**NASB** – New American Standard Bible
**ESV** – English Standard Version
**KVJ** – King James Version

**All For The Prize Publications**

www.actschristianity.org

"Go into all the world and proclaim the Gospel to all creation...and these signs will follow those who believe..."

> —The Lord Jesus, The Great Commission
> (Mark 16:15, 17)

"And they went out and proclaimed everywhere, the Lord working with them and confirming the message with accompanying signs" (Mark 16:20)

> —Action & result of His first disciples
> (Mark 16:20)

# Foreword

On the morning of January 13th, 2017, my friend and travel companion, Tom, excitedly greeted me on the shore of Lake Victoria in southern Uganda. We had arrived the night before. "Last night God wouldn't let me sleep!" He told me. He grabbed my arms excitedly as he told me how God kept leading him to Jeremiah 33:3 and 6:

**3 Call to Me [the LORD], and I will answer you, and show you great and mighty things, which you do not know... 6 Behold, I will bring it health and healing; I will heal them and reveal to them the abundance of peace and truth. (Jeremiah 33:3, 6)**

"God's gonna heal people and show me things I don't know!!" He yelled excitedly. I shared his excitement, knowing that God would do just that.

We proceeded to northern Uganda where we evangelized, and taught/trained some of God's precious people. I remember one disciple, after being healed miraculously, asked Tom and I to go to her house with her to bring God's healing to her sick son. It was too far. "After the training," I told her, "you will be able to go and heal him in Jesus Name." Several days later, she did just that, and she returned to tell us about it.

Some of the women really enjoyed my wife, her look being so different and her countenance so kind. One sister requested help with her HIV. About a year later, when Tom went back, he witnessed that all of her symptoms were still gone. She had been healed by Jesus.

There were too many miraculous healings to count. In the last meeting, we asked if there was anyone who still had sickness and invited them to come to the front. A woman came up who was healed the first day. I asked what she wanted. It was *not* to be prayed for; she wanted to give healing to others who would come up.

After we left, some from the group we trained went to a hospital and laid hands on everyone there. The next day, when they went back, they found only a few patients left. The others had gone home healed! I told them, "Make them into disciples." *This is the goal.*

We went on from there to another city. When praying with our host the first night, he spoke twice by the Spirit, "Call unto me and I will show you great and marvelous things that you have not known" (Jer 33:3). He knew nothing of what God told Tom. The next morning, in the meeting, another brother, unaware of these things, opened the meeting by proclaiming the same verse to the people and then repeating it.

That afternoon I sat in silence before God and received an outline of what to teach: "Healing Training." God confirmed his Word with signs following, the Lord doing His work alongside of us as we went out. Everyone had testimonies. In fact, after one outreach session, the teams were giving reports of sharing the Gospel and of miracles. Eventually I stood up to start teaching again, but the translator sat me down. He hadn't shared of the miracles he saw yet!

One lady's foot was instantly healed so she could jump up and down for joy. After a little training, she was in the market and gave God's healing to a woman there, boldly. She also testified to us that she had always been despised in her family, and she said, "I never imagined that *I* could heal the sick."

Part way through the week, I was, again, sitting silently before God. I heard him clearly speak to me to write this training into a book. I was astonished, as I never would've have imagined doing so. This is it.

I encourage you to now call unto Him and ask him to show you great things you don't know, unto miraculous healing and health for you and others.

# Contents

Foreword..................................................iv

1. Know Our History.................................1

2. What Does Healing Require?..................3

3. Do You Have Authority to Heal?............10

4. Who Does the Healing? Who Casts Out the Demon?..................................................14

5. How Do You Heal? Answer: Like Jesus...............19

6. Role of Prayer in Healing.......................25

7. The Mind of Christ................................33

8. At Times, Find the Cause......................36

Recommended Resources.........................39

# Chapter 1: Know Our History

When Jesus walked the earth He served as an example for us. As the great Teacher, He taught and trained His disciples on healing, and He left his Words for us to read and learn from today. We've missed this because we've generally only seen Him as the Savior and Lord and not as the Teacher. I believe Matthew through Acts is the greatest manual on God's healing.

God's People eventually lost the truths Jesus taught his first students ("disciples"). Tradition came in which provided an alternative way of the Christian "religion," and mixture with the world came in. These two things stopped faith among God's holy People, so miraculous healing stopped (See Mark 7:8-13, 6:5-6; James 1:6-7).

Then false doctrines were formed to explain why the healing stopped because man makes his present state the standard. This is done out of pride. What he has must be the best there is because it's what he has.

The Bible was eventually concealed from all but a few select people in Europe, "the clergy." In the 1500s, Martin Luther and William Tyndale translated the Bible into modern languages, so the masses could read it. Right around this time the printing press was invented, so the Bible could be spread far and wide. This started a mental and spiritual restoration for God's People. We've been recovering lost truths ever since. The Spirit of Truth has been leading us into them.

Around the early 1900s many people discovered Bible truths about healing and miracles. These individuals used their new found knowledge to travel and help thousands of people.

So what was Satan's counterattack? One aspect of it was prestige. I believe he tempted those with knowledge of their power, to enjoy the spotlight rather than teach others to do the same. Others did try to empower all to do the same, but they found themselves held up on a pedestal by the people.

Various mental strongholds of the enemy followed:

- Only "special" people can heal the sick (for the Truth see Acts 3:12, 2Peter 1:1, Mark 16:17-18, John 14:12, Acts 1:8). Satan spread this doctrine because if Jesus is unable to use His whole Body to heal the sick, He won't be able to heal all He wants to
- Having or using faith is difficult (See Mt 11:28-30)
- Sicknesses are typically God teaching us a lesson. He wants us to bear them, so we should value them (See Acts 10:38, Luke 13:16, Mark 7:27, Exodus 15:26)
- Miracles only happened in the past (See Mk 16:15-16; Mt 28:18-20, 21:21-22; 1Cor 1:4-8, 13:10-12)
- Miracles only happen in other, far away places (See Mk 16:20, Mt 28:19, Lk 24:47-49, Acts 1:8)
- Healing miracles makes the *person* God uses great (See Acts 3:12, 14:15)

Satan also counterattacked by sending total counterfeits who "taught healing" for money or glory. These weren't just tempted by prestige. They were wolves in sheep's clothing. The result of their work included terribly disappointing people and often blaming people for their "lack of faith." As all who sin against us, these people must be forgiven.

Please take a moment to get quiet before God and ask him to bring up anyone who has wounded you in the past in this area. If this has happened, thoroughly forgive the person and start fresh in this area, in your soul. Give as much time as you need to do this before coming back to this book.

Among other things, Satan's counterattack on this aspect of the Word of God has resulted in a wrong mindset. This mindset has caused many of God's People, when sick, to explain "why I can't be healed by God," instead of seeking, "How can I be healed by God?"

# Chapter 2
# What Does Healing Require?

I'm going to cover several requirements, listed in Scripture, for miracles. These are not all, always required, and this is not an exhaustive list. These are some of the basic requirements.

1. Faith

First of all, without a doubt, FAITH brings about God's miraculous healing:

**Jesus said to him, "If you can believe, all things are possible to him who believes." (Mark 9:23, NKJV)**

This can be on the part of the person receiving healing or on the part those helping that person. About 50% of the time, when Jesus healed people he told them, "Your faith has made you well." He was teaching them, and he was encouraging them to keep believing in Him and in God. More problems would come their way. If they could learn that it was their faith that made them well that time, they could keep using faith to access God's help in the future.

How did their faith make them well? It brought them to Jesus, the Healer. When the lame man's friends lowered him through a hole in the roof where Jesus was, he saw *their faith*. He saw the great efforts they made to get to Him—it clearly showed they had faith in Him to heal the man.

Faith does not always have to be on the part of the person who's receiving healing. For example:

**"And He [Jesus] said to them, "Go into all the world and preach the gospel to all creation...These signs will**

accompany those who have believed...they will lay hands on the sick, and they will recover." **(Mark 16:15-17, NASB)**

Here we see a picture of believers going and laying hands on the sick and the sick recovering. This verse is primarily in the context of evangelism—going to *unbelievers*. You can't expect un-believers to believe! This is just one example, and there are others in Scripture.

It's *our* job to believe when we go. Jesus loves faith in people. It pleases him. But many who we need to help may not know and have faith in God's Word. We can help them with that, if they're open. Or we can believe *for* them, if they're willing to let us. Eventually they should also hear Truth so they can believe. We also need to keep growing in our own knowledge and belief in God's Word.

How did the people in Jesus day *get faith*? Romans 10:17 teaches, "Faith comes through hearing, and hearing by a spoken Word of God" (Literal). So they heard about JESUS, and when they did, God was speaking to them also, and they believed. This faith then led them to Him. ☺ Also whenever he taught, they were "hearing" and could then believe.

We must maintain the same child-like heart, to listen, to hear God, to go to where Jesus is speaking in order to "complete what is lacking in [our] faith" (1Thes 3:10). There's always more that he wants to teach us.

2. Not doubting

Jesus commended faith. He taught, "All things are possible to those who believe," and he also helped humble people with their unbelief (Mark 9:23-24). Unbelief, doubt, and fear seek to stop the immense power of God that works through our faith.

**Then Jesus answered and said, "O faithless and perverse generation, how long shall I be with you? How long shall I bear with you? Bring him here to Me." 18 And Jesus rebuked the demon, and it came out of him; and the child**

was cured from that very hour. 19 Then the disciples came to Jesus privately and said, "Why could we not cast it out?" 20 So Jesus said to them, "Because of your unbelief; for assuredly, I say to you, if you have faith as a mustard seed, you will say to this mountain, 'Move from here to there,' and it will move; and nothing will be impossible for you. (Matthew 17:17-20, NKJV)

Notice that unbelief, based on the physical circumstances for example, can *cancel out* the faith in our heart.

These same disciples had gone out previously to "heal the sick, cleanse the lepers, raise the dead, cast out demons" (Mt 10:8). *They had faith!* They were surprised they couldn't cast out the demon this time, so they asked about it. Jesus said it was their unbelief. Apparently, the dramatic scene the boy displayed pulled them out of their faith into unbelief. So we must deal with unbelief at times to stay in faith—the faith that we already have.

Jesus did not say they *needed more faith*. He put the emphasis on dealing with unbelief.

We must guard our minds from unbelief and from fear-filled words. Jesus helped a synagogue ruler to continue on the path of his faith when he was delivered bad news:

**While He [Jesus] was still speaking, someone came from the ruler of the synagogue's [house], saying to him, "Your daughter is dead. Do not trouble the Teacher." 50 But when Jesus heard [it], He answered him, saying, "Do not be afraid;** *only believe***, and she will be made well." (Luke 8:49-50, NKJV; emphasis mine)**

The enemy was trying to spread fear to the man who Jesus was seeking to help. Jesus encouraged him to block out fear and "only believe." This was the hard part for him at that time. In the same way, staying free from fear and unbelief requires the constant discipline of blocking out the world's ideas. It requires a lifestyle of always using a fine filter.

**Does not the ear test words as the palate tastes food? (Job 12:11)**

Just as "faith comes by hearing" the Word of God, unbelief comes by listening to the word of unbelievers. "Death and life are in the power of the tongue" (Prov 18:21).

Theological training is not necessarily "hearing the spoken Word of God." Sometimes it's listening to man. Sometimes it builds sophisticated strongholds of unbelief in the minds of its hearers. Its after effect can be excruciating. The greatest counterfeit is always the one closest to the truth. It has always benefitted my soul to *run* from theology when its not infused with the Word of God Himself.

It's not enough to believe, we also have to block out unbelief, fear, and to not doubt—to "only believe."

**So Jesus answered and said to them, "Assuredly, I say to you, if you have faith *and do not doubt*, you will not only do what was done to the fig tree, but also if you say to this mountain, 'Be removed and be cast into the sea,' it will be done. (Matthew 21:21, NASB; emphasis mine)**

**But if any of you lacks wisdom, let him ask of God, who gives to all generously and without reproach, and it will be given to him. 6 But he must ask in faith *without any doubting*, for the one who doubts is like the surf of the sea, driven and tossed by the wind. 7 For that man ought not to expect that he will receive anything from the Lord, 8 [being] a double-minded man, unstable in all his ways. (James 1:5-8, NASB; emphasis mine)**

Physical circumstances and conditions will try pull us out of the faith in our heart, into doubt, fear, unbelief. So the battle is to keep the truths of the Word of God before our eyes so that we see them as more relevant than the circumstances (Prov 4:20-21, Romans 4:19). This is "fighting the good fight of faith" (1Tim 6:12).

And in the fourth watch of the night He [Jesus] came to them, walking on the sea. 26 When the disciples saw Him walking on the sea, they were terrified, and said, "It is a ghost!" And they cried out in fear. 27 But immediately Jesus spoke to them, saying, "Take courage, it is I; do not be afraid." 28 Peter said to Him, "Lord, if it is You, command me to come to You on the water." 29 And He said, "Come!" And Peter got out of the boat, and walked on the water and came toward Jesus. 30 But seeing the wind, he became frightened, and beginning to sink, he cried out, "Lord, save me!" 31 Immediately Jesus stretched out His hand and took hold of him, and said to him, "You of little faith, why did you doubt?" 32 When they got into the boat, the wind stopped. (Matthew 14:25-32, NASB)

Jesus words to Peter were, literally, "Little faith, unto what did you doubt?" He was helping him consider and pinpoint what it was that caused him to doubt, so he could go past that in the future.

When we hear and believe the Word of God in an area, we then have faith in that area. After that we must be careful to manage our souls and "keep faith" (1Tim 1:19)—guarding our hearts, being careful what we let in, taking much time with God and the Truth. This is how Jesus lived, and we're called to do so also.

Lastly, a HUGE help against the unbelief, fear and doubting which is based on our five physical senses, is *fasting and prayer*.

3. Action

Another thing that's necessary for healing, many times, is *action*.

**For as the body without the spirit is dead, so faith without works is dead also. (James 2:26, NKJV)**

This verse is saying, in other words, that there are two kinds of faith. There is faith that is alive, and there is faith that is dead. You can have *great* faith, but without action it is *dead*. But when we take action, combined with our faith, our faith is *alive*, and it's working. And the miracle can happen.

This are obviously not "works of the law" which do not require faith (Gal 3:12). This is working based on the faith we receive in our hearts as we hear Truth.

4. Love

Paul said it's possible to have faith that can move mountains but not love (1Cor 13:2). He said if that is you, you "are nothing." So as we grow in faith we must guard our hearts and make sure we have love. The Bible says all that matters is "faith that works through love" (Gal 5:6).

We have God's love in your heart, and we must allow it to flourish through continuously receiving God's Word and obeying it, and that love will cause us to reach out to people. It will cause us to ask, "How are you? Do you need help? Can I pray with you?" Otherwise, you can have faith in your heart that you can "lay hands on the sick and they shall recover," for example. But that faith will not work because you're not loving anyone.

5. Jesus

I love this one. Healing requires Jesus! Jesus said, "apart from Me you can do nothing" (John 15:5). He also said, "I speak the words, and my Father does the works" (John 14:9). It's the same for us, but in our case Jesus does the works.

So along with all that I'm teaching you, the way to grow in this is relationship with Jesus, growing in reliance on Jesus. Jesus, the greatest miracle worker who ever lived on earth, said,

**"Most assuredly, I say to you, the Son can do nothing of Himself, but what He sees the Father do; for whatever He**

does, the Son also does in like manner. 20 "For the Father loves the Son, and shows Him all things that He Himself does; and He will show Him greater works than these, that you may marvel. (John 5:19-20, NKJV)

We don't want to do miracles and help people *apart* from Jesus. By the help of the Holy Spirit, we can do things exactly how he wants. We can be in the right place, at the right time, speaking the right words, in His Name, and watching Him do the works he wants through us.

6. Sometimes *persistence*

Miraculous healing doesn't always happen instantly. There can be a "fight of faith"! Our faith will be tested. During these times, we must apply persistence and endurance to our faith.

**And we desire that each one of you show the same diligence so as to realize the full assurance of hope until the end, 12 so that you will not be sluggish, but imitators of those who through faith and patience inherit the promises. (Hebrews 6:11-12; NASB)**

Our father of faith, Abraham, persisted in believing for years and eventually received the miraculous birth of Isaac.
Scripture describes an occasion in which Jesus healed a blind man. I love Mark 8:22-25 because these verses show *how* Jesus did it. We'll look at it more in detail later, but the first time Jesus laid hands on the man, he wasn't healed completely. He had to do it twice for his full healing. He didn't *give up* halfway saying, "It doesn't work," "I don't have enough faith," or "It must not be God's will." He persisted.
As Jesus' disciples, we should become the most persistent people on earth.

# Chapter 3
# Do You Have Authority to Heal?

"God will do what you cannot do, but he won't do what you can do. And if we do what we can do, God will do what we can't do."
"God wants to do stuff *through* you not just *for* you."
— Joyce Meyer

And Jesus came up and spoke to them, saying, "All authority has been given to Me in heaven and on earth. 19 "Go therefore and make disciples of all the nations, baptizing them[,] in the name of the Father and the Son and the Holy Spirit, 20 teaching them to observe all that I commanded you; and lo, I am with you [every day], even to the end of the age." (Matthew 28:18-20, NASB)

Jesus gave this original commission to the followers He had left at the time of His ascension. *It included a perpetual factor*, teaching them to observe ALL THAT I COMMANDED YOU. This means that the teaching we have of Jesus is for each disciple today, including this commission to go make disciples.
Mark's Gospel tells more of *how* to do the job:

And He said to them, "Go into all the world and preach the gospel to all creation. 16 "He who has believed and has been baptized shall be saved; but he who has disbelieved shall be condemned. 17 "These signs will accompany those who have believed: in My name they will cast out demons, they will speak with new tongues; 18 they will pick up serpents, and if they drink any deadly poison, it will not hurt them; they will lay hands on the sick, and they will recover." 19 So then, when the Lord Jesus had spoken to them, He was received up into heaven and sat down at the right hand of God. 20 And they went out and preached everywhere, while the Lord worked with them, and confirmed the word by the signs that followed. (Mark 16:15-20, NASB)

Jesus had already trained them to heal the sick and cast out demons, by faith. He had served as an example for them, and He had sent them out to do it already:

and heal those in it who are sick, and say to them, 'The kingdom of God has come near to you.' (Luke 10:9, NASB)

By sending them *to do it*, the Master had given them authority to do it. We share this same authority. What we may lack are *knowledge* and *training*.

Everything in the first four Gospels applies to us, including this next promise. According to the context, the "works" he spoke of here clearly refer to miracles:

"Truly, truly, I say to you, he who believes in Me, the works that I do, he will do also; and greater works than these he will do; because I go to the Father. (John 14:12, NASB)

In my opinion, the greater works are leading a person to Jesus to receive the new birth, and helping someone receive immersion in the Holy Spirit. Jesus never did these things before His cross. They are left for us to do with Him now. And we have authority and power to do the same works Jesus did on earth: heal the sick, cleanse lepers, raise the dead, heal "all manner of sickness and disease," expel demons from people (Mt 4:23, 9:35).

**Jesus summoned His twelve disciples and gave them authority over unclean spirits, to cast them out, and to heal every kind of disease and every kind of sickness. (Matthew 10:1, NASB)**

These twelve Jesus sent out and commanded them, saying: 7 "...as you go, preach, saying, 'The kingdom of heaven is [near].' 8 "Heal the sick, cleanse the lepers, raise the dead, cast out demons. Freely you have received, freely give. (Matthew 10:5, 7-8; NKJV)

This authority works by faith and with the help of the Holy Spirit. We *have* the authority already, and we are to be learning to use it, as the early disciples were.

When we know that we have authority by the One who sent us into the world, we can then begin to use it. YOU HAVE BEEN AUTHORIZED TO HEAL—all manner of sickness and disease. If Satan can get us to doubt that, we won't use it. But if we believe it as a child, we can exercise it.

Authority and power work together. God has given us power:

Now He said to them, "These are My words which I spoke to you while I was still with you, that all things which are written about Me in the Law of Moses and the Prophets and the Psalms must be fulfilled." 45 Then He opened their minds to understand the Scriptures, 46 and He said to them, "Thus it is written, that the Christ would suffer and rise again from the dead the third day, 47 and that repentance for forgiveness of sins would be proclaimed in His name to all the nations, beginning from Jerusalem. 48 "You are witnesses of these things. 49 "And behold, I am sending forth the promise of My Father upon you; but you are to stay in the city until you are clothed with power from on high." (Luke 24:44-49, NASB)

You will receive power when the Holy Spirit has come upon you; and you shall be My witnesses both in Jerusalem, and in all Judea and Samaria, and even to the remotest part of the earth." (Acts 1:8, NASB)

If you have received immersion in the Holy Spirit, *you have this power!*

Paul and the other apostles prayed that our eyes be opened to the immeasurable power that is already toward us (See Eph 1:15-23). They wanted us to be strengthened with power, more and more, by the Holy Spirit *who is already in us!* (Eph 3:16). *We don't need more power.* What we need is more and more revelation and to use what we already have, in Messiah! (1Cor 2:12, Philemon vs 6).

# Chapter 4
# Who Does the Healing?
# Who Casts Out the Demon?

We want our thinking to be shaped by the Scripture. What does the Scripture say about this?

In one sense, WE do it *through* the Messiah's authority:

[Jesus commanded:] heal those in [the town] who are sick, and say to them, 'The kingdom of God has come near to you.' (Luke 10:9, NASB)

And these signs will follow those who believe in My name: they will cast out demons; they will speak with new tongues. (Mark 16:17)

A bigger picture reveals that what actually heals is Jesus' name (authority), faith in His name, and His power and piety (godliness). We get to be willing participants, and HE does miracles *through* us.

But Peter said, "I do not possess silver and gold, but what I do have I give to you: In the name of Jesus Christ the Nazarene--walk!" 7 And seizing him by the right hand, he raised him up; and immediately his feet and his ankles were strengthened. 8 With a leap he stood upright and began to walk; and he entered the temple with them, walking and leaping and praising God. 9 And all the people saw him walking and praising God; 10 and they were taking note of him as being the one who used to sit at the Beautiful Gate of the temple to beg alms, and they were filled with wonder and amazement at what had happened to him. 11 While he was clinging to Peter and

John, all the people ran together to them at the so-called portico of Solomon, full of amazement. 12 But when Peter saw this, he replied to the people, "Men of Israel, why are you amazed at this, or why do you gaze at us, as if by our own power or piety we had made him walk?...16 His name, through faith in His name, has made this man strong, whom you see and know. Yes, the faith which comes through Him has given him this perfect soundness in the presence of you all. (Acts 3:6-12, 16, NKJV)

Later, about the same miracle, Peter said:

"If we this day are judged for a good deed done to a helpless man, by what means he has been made well, let it be known to you all, and to all the people of Israel, that by the name of Jesus Christ of Nazareth, whom you crucified, whom God raised from the dead, by Him this man stands here before you whole." (Acts 4:9-10).

Here's another one. Bro. Paul said,

For I will not venture to speak of anything except what Christ has accomplished through me to bring the Gentiles to obedience--by word and deed, 19 by the power of signs and wonders, by the power of the Spirit of God (Romans 15:18-19, ESV)

Why "through us"? The Messiah has chosen to bind Himself to us, to give us the dignity of serving as His Body. We are "co-laborers" with Him (1Cor 3:9, Mt 11:29, 1Thes 3:2). God wants to glorify us with Him (2Thes 1:11-12), and He has already glorified us in Him spiritually (Ro 8:30). We are His holy temple.

In Old Covenant times, when people wanted to get near to God, they would go to His temple in Israel. Now, we have been made His temple. He lives in us! When people want Him,

15

they can come to us, and He can heal them through us. When we go to people, we are bringing the almighty, holy presence of God with us to them!

What race or skin color is Jesus?

When Jesus rose, those joined to Him through faith in the Gospel became His Body. So His current race includes all of the people who have believed in Him: black, white, brown, red, yellow...He lives in each of us.

In Acts 9:4, Jesus said to Paul/Saul: "Saul, Saul, why are you persecuting me?" Saul had been attacking and "breathing threats and murder against the disciples of the Lord" (Acts 8:1-3, 9:1). But Jesus said, "You are persecuting Me." The Lord and we are one.

**Now you are the body of Christ... (1Corinthians 12:27, NKJV)**

Jesus has chosen to limit Himself to you. He wants to shine through you, as His image. He's chosen to reach out to people through you, His Body. He wants to work through you, to serve through your serving, to heal through you, to speak through you.

The whole point of this age is for us who've believed to be joined with Him, co-laboring with Jesus as His Body, being trained and serving with Him, being conformed into His image.

God's redemption, in the Messiah Jesus, was so thorough that having forgiven us all past sins and having cleansed our spirits completely, that He can actually live in us and function through us.

**In Him we have redemption through His blood, the forgiveness of sins, according to the riches of His grace (Ephesians 1:7, NKJV)**

...you were washed, but you were sanctified [set apart], but you were justified [made righteous] in the name of the Lord Jesus and by the Spirit of our God. (1Corinthians

6:11, NKJV)

For you are the temple of the living God. (2Corinthians 6:16, NKJV)

This is very different than in the Old Covenant. God's People would go to the temple to seek Him and call on Him. They'd seek to get near Him. We now, having been brought near already through the blood of His Son, *carry Him*. He goes through us to others.

Another thing to keep in mind:

**God has chosen the foolish things of the world to shame the wise, and God has chosen the weak things of the world to shame the things which are strong, 28 and the base things of the world and the despised God has chosen, the things that are not, so He may nullify the things that are (1Corinthians 1:27-28, NASB)**

God uses weak people, so that He's glorified. He uses us. We should not try to become perfect or strong in human strength, trying to get God to use us. Right now, where we're at—weak—he'll use us.

God is more stubborn than humans, and He's right. If we try to go about receiving or giving healing in ways other than His New Covenant ways, we may stubbornly die trying. It's not that He does not love us, but His ways are set. It's we that must seek and find them, humbly.

Consider again Romans 15:18-19, listed out above. Paul said he wouldn't talk about anything other than what the Messiah did through him.... I used to not talk about miracles when I would see them. I was somehow trained to downplay them, to not talk about them as if it would make me proud or something (?). That was a mistake. Paul talked about miracles:

**Then all the multitude kept silent and listened to Barnabas and Paul declaring how many miracles and**

wonders God had worked through them among the Gentiles. (Acts 15:12, NKJV)

When he had greeted them [James and all the elders], he told in detail those things which God had done among the Gentiles through his ministry. 20 And when they heard [it], they glorified the Lord... (Acts 21:19-20, NKJV)

**Declare His glory among the nations, His wonders [Or, "marvelous works"] among all peoples. (Psalm 96:3, NKJV)**

Talk about them! Glorify Him! He did the miracles. He wants and deserves glory! Give glory to Him for the works He does through us!

Talking about miracles "spreads Jesus' fame." It also raises people's expectation. Positive expectation is the meaning of "hope" in the Bible. It has been called "the womb of miracles." Expectation and faith work together.

Nowadays I talk about the miracles I experience and see, always careful to glorify the God who did them through us. I surround myself with others who value God's wonders and talk about them continually also.

# 5. How Do You Heal? Answer: Like Jesus

Jesus said about His disciples:

**A pupil is not above his teacher; but everyone, after he has been fully trained, will be like his teacher. (Luke 6:40, NASB)**

This is the goal. We're in training to become like our Teacher. The Bible calls Jesus "Master" about 40 times in the KJV. The accurate translation, at least today, would be "Teacher." He is our Teacher. He's training us—to be like Him, the greatest privilege of all.

He also said,

**Do you not believe that I am in the Father, and the Father is in Me? The words that I say to you I do not speak on My own initiative, but the Father abiding in Me does His works. 11 Believe Me that I am in the Father and the Father is in Me; otherwise believe because of the works themselves. 12 Truly, truly, I say to you, he who believes in Me, the works that I do, he will do also; and greater works than these he will do; because I go to the Father. (John 14:10-12, NASB)**

Jesus miracles were done *as He was doing the will of the Father*. He said, "My food is to do the will of the One who sent me, and to finish His work" (John 4:34). This driving, heart's desire of Jesus is to be shared in us now. We must be going forward toward completing the Great Commission Jesus gave us. "Go into all the world and preach...these signs will follow...and Lo, I am with you every day to the end of the age."

It should be in our veins to help fulfill this Great

Commission. We should never feel our work is finished till this is finished.

Jesus calmed storms, walked on water, fed multitudes—all while doing the Father's work. He was on His way to doing the will of God when needs and problems arose that he miraculously fixed. We must be also.

How else did Jesus do His miracles? Routinely, he got up early in the mornings to pray. He spent time with His Father, and then he came down to where people were and healed them by faith.

There are several prayers of Jesus recorded in Scripture, but none in Scripture in which He prayed for the Father to heal or cast demons out of people. Jesus knew He had authority to do these miracles, given to Him by the Father who sent Him. He was leaving an example for us (1Pe 2:21, 1Cor 11:1, Eph 5:1).

**"And these signs will follow those who believe: In My name they will cast out demons…18…they will lay hands on the sick, and they will recover." (Mark 16:17-18, NKJV)**

Jesus typically healed the sick by command and by the laying on of hands. For example,

…a leper came and worshiped Him, saying, "Lord, if You are willing, You can make me clean." 3 Then Jesus put out [His] hand and touched him, saying, "I am willing; be cleansed." Immediately his leprosy was cleansed. (Matthew 8:2-3, NKJV)

13 Then Jesus said to the centurion, "Go your way; and as you have believed, [so] let it be done for you." And his servant was healed that same hour. 14 Now when Jesus had come into Peter's house, He saw his wife's mother lying sick with a fever. 15 So He touched her hand, and the fever left her. And she arose and served them. 16 When evening had come, they brought to Him many who were

[demonized]. And He cast out the spirits with a word, and healed all who were sick (Matthew 8:13-16, NASB)

In verse 13, notice how Jesus healed the centurion's servant: "Let it be done...." He declared or commanded it. He exercised his authority with words. In verse 14 he "touched her hand, and the fever left her"—the laying on of hands. These are patterns for us.

This parallel passage gives us a more complete picture:

Then He got up and left the synagogue, and entered Simon's home. Now Simon's mother-in-law was suffering from a high fever, and they asked Him to help her. 39 And standing over her, He rebuked the fever, and it left her; and she immediately got up and waited on them. 40 While the sun was setting, all those who had any who were sick with various diseases brought them to Him; and laying His hands on each one of them, He was healing them. (Luke 4:38-40, NASB)

So he used both a command and physical touch to heal Simon's mother-in-law. And we see that He used the laying on of hands to heal "all who were sick" who came to him that night.

Jesus taught His disciples along these lines:

Now in the morning, as they passed by, they saw the fig tree dried up from the roots. 21 And Peter, remembering, said to Him, "Rabbi, look! The fig tree which You cursed has withered away." 22 So Jesus answered and said to them, "Have faith in God.[1] 23 "For assuredly, I say to you, whoever says to this mountain, 'Be removed and be cast into the sea,' and does not doubt in his heart, but believes

---

[1] Literally, "HAVE FAITH GOD." Maybe, "Have faith in God," or "Have faith of God," or "Have faith like God." God created the ages by faith, through His spoken command (Heb 11:3, Gen 1:3; see also Rom 4:17).

that those things he says will be done, he will have whatever he says. (Mark 11:20-23, NKJV)

Here He was teaching one way that faith works—by command. If there is a problem to be solved, Jesus said to *speak to it*, to command it. It will obey us if we believe and don't doubt in our hearts. There is a category of things that we are to speak to like this, and sickness and demons are included—as Jesus did.

Jesus' early students ("disciples") followed their Teacher's example and teaching:

**But Peter said, "I do not possess silver and gold, but what I do have I give to you: In the name of Jesus Christ the Nazarene--walk!" 7 And seizing him by the right hand, he raised him up; and immediately his feet and his ankles were strengthened. 8 With a leap he stood upright and began to walk... (Acts 3:6-8, NKJV)**

They used what they possessed. Freely they had received, so freely they gave (Mt 10:8). Here, Peter gave healing to this crippled man by command and the laying on of hands, through faith and the understanding of his authority.

While teaching this course and evangelizing in the evening, a man came to me and showed me his ankle. One side was swollen about twice the normal size. It had been in pain for years. I laid hands on his ankle, knowing fully that the Messiah is in *me* now and wanted to heal him. I waited a bit and just allowed the Messiah to do His work, not saying anything. I stayed in the faith that I had. Then we looked and saw that it was normal sized, and all the pain was gone.

Here's an example of Paul healing the sick:

**...there they continued to preach the gospel. [notice that, like Jesus, they were doing their job]. 8 At Lystra a man was sitting who had no strength in his feet, lame from his mother's womb, who had never walked. 9 This man was listening to Paul as he spoke, who, when he had fixed his**

gaze on him and had seen that he had faith to be made well, 10 said with a loud voice, "Stand upright on your feet." And he leaped up and began to walk. (Acts 14:7-10, NASB)

In this case, Paul saw that the man had faith to be healed. The Spirit may have opened his eyes to it. What did Paul do next? Did he ask God to heal the man? No. He commanded the man to stand. In doing so, he was using his authority and also helping the man add action to his faith, making it alive and powerful.

How else did Jesus heal? Mark 8 describes Jesus healing a blind man. God gives us a detailed picture here, to help us:

**And they came to Bethsaida. And they brought a blind man to Jesus and implored Him to touch him. 23 Taking the blind man by the hand, He brought him out of the village; and after spitting on his eyes and laying His hands on him, He asked him, "Do you see anything?" 24 And he looked up and said, "I see men, for I see them like trees, walking around." 25 Then again He laid His hands on his eyes; and he looked intently and was restored, and began to see everything clearly. (Mark 8:22-25, NASB)**

Notice in verse 22 that they wanted Jesus to touch him. Jesus was healing the sick through the laying on of hands so often that they believed it would happen that way. In this case, Jesus

1) Laid hands on him
2) Asked him about his improvement
3) When he heard the man needed more healing, he laid hands on him again, till he was totally healed

My wife and I laid hands on an elderly disciple who was walking very slowly and depending on a walking stick. We commanded her leg to heal and then asked her to try it out. She was a bit better. So we did it again, and again, and again, and again. We spent about 20 minutes with her, and in the end, she could walk fast, without the stick.

On another occasion, we laid hands on a woman who was virtually deaf in one ear. We did not stop because of partial or seemingly no improvement. We persisted, and in the end, after about 15 minutes, she could hear very well in that ear, the same as in the other.

Three of us were asked to help another friend of mine's mother. She had just gotten back from the doctor and was given two medications for her knee. The doctor reported that she had little or no cartilage left there. We could hear the knee click when she walked. We spent what seemed like a long time, laying on hands and commanding her healing. It healed. God may have grown new cartilage there. No more pain or clicking.

In John chapter 5 Jesus approached a sick man and asked him, "Do you want to be well?" By this example, we can also go to people and ask if they have sickness or pain and if they want to be healed. If they allow us, we can then command their healing and/or lay hands on them, and they will recover. This typically opens the door to tell them the Good News about the Messiah. This is one, clear, Scriptural way of evangelism (see Luke 10:9).

In male/female interactions, it is sometimes not fitting or tactful to lay hands on the person. When going out, in some cases, I will simply *point* to the problem area and command it. God will heal through you the same way. This is important because as God's People, we should be known for the highest integrity and discretion.

Find a sick person now, and put your faith in these things into action. Then tell about the miracles that result. Tell the right people, "careful not to cast your pearls before swine." Keep doing it and telling about it, and your expectation will grow. You've already been equipped enough to do a lot. Go….

# Chapter 6
# Role of Prayer in Healing

If Jesus said to "Speak to the mountain," what is the role of prayer in healing? Let's look into the Scriptures.

When Jesus raised Lazarus from the dead, he prayed, but not for the actual raising:

>...Then Jesus raised His eyes, and said, "Father, I thank You that You have heard Me. 42 "I knew that You always hear Me; but because of the people standing around I said it, so that they may believe that You sent Me." 43 When He had said these things, He cried out with a loud voice, "Lazarus, come forth." (John 11:41-43, NASB)

Notice that He prayed, in this case, for the people around Him to hear it and believe in Him. Last week, I also prayed similarly before giving healing to a man in the name of Jesus. I said loudly, "So that those standing around may know that you sent Jesus and that he gave himself up on the cross for them and you raised him from the dead!" then I commanded his healing. The next day there was so much of an improvement in his condition that one of the unbelievers who had seen it acknowledged it was a miracle.

Jesus typically prayed in the mornings and then served the People. We are to do likewise. We serve, in His Name, in His stead, in His authority, with Him. We use the authority vested in us as his co-laborers sent out in His name, confidently and in faith.

Here's an example from Peter's work:

>Now as Peter was traveling through all those regions, he came down also to the saints who lived at Lydda. 33 There he found a man named Aeneas, who had been bedridden

eight years, for he was paralyzed. 34 Peter said to him, "Aeneas, Jesus Christ heals you; get up and make your bed." Immediately he got up. 35 And all who lived at Lydda and Sharon saw him, and they turned to the Lord. 36 Now in Joppa there was a disciple named Tabitha (which translated in Greek is called Dorcas); this woman was abounding with deeds of kindness and charity which she continually did. 37 And it happened at that time that she fell sick and died; and when they had washed her body, they laid it in an upper room. 38 Since Lydda was near Joppa, the disciples, having heard that Peter was there, sent two men to him, imploring him, "Do not delay in coming to us." 39 So Peter arose and went with them. When he arrived, they brought him into the upper room; and all the widows stood beside him, weeping and showing all the tunics and garments that Dorcas used to make while she was with them. 40 But Peter sent them all out and knelt down and prayed, and turning to the body, he said, "Tabitha, arise." And she opened her eyes, and when she saw Peter, she sat up. 41 And he gave her his hand and raised her up; and calling the saints and widows, he presented her alive. 42 It became known all over Joppa, and many believed in the Lord. (Acts 9:32-42, NASB)

In verse 40, we see that Peter prayed first. What was he praying? I can imagine him lining himself up with the Lord and His Truth, clearing his mind, asking for mercy and help to do his job well. We do know what came next: he used his God given authority to command her to arise. He stood boldly in faith and did the job, depending on Jesus in him.

Jesus had sent him: "...raise the dead..." (Mt 10:8), just as He has sent us. Peter didn't doubt his authority and beg Jesus to do the job. He had been trained, so he stood, in Jesus' stead, and commanded it to happen. And Jesus was then able to raise her.

Similar to Peter above, Paul brought healing to a man this

way:

> And it happened that the father of Publius lay sick of a fever and dysentery. Paul went in to him and prayed, and he laid his hands on him and healed him. So when this was done, the rest of those on the island who had diseases also came and were healed. (Acts 28:8-9, NKJV)

We can do the same.

Here's another example of prayer first, then healing. Ananias was not an apostle, like Peter or Paul. We don't have to be. Jesus said the signs would follow those who believe, and the works He did would be done by those who believe.

> Now there was a certain disciple at Damascus named Ananias; and to him the Lord said in a vision, "Ananias." And he said, "Here I am, Lord." 11 So the Lord [said] to him, "Arise and go to the street called Straight, and inquire at the house of Judas for [one] called Saul of Tarsus, for behold, he is praying. 12 And in a vision he has seen a man named Ananias coming in and putting [his] hand on him, so that he might receive his sight." 13 Then Ananias answered, "Lord, I have heard from many about this man, how much harm he has done to Your saints in Jerusalem. 14 And here he has authority from the chief priests to bind all who call on Your name." 15 But the Lord said to him, "Go, for he is a chosen vessel of Mine to bear My name before Gentiles, kings, and the children of Israel. 16 For I will show him how many things he must suffer for My name's sake." 17 And Ananias went his way and entered the house; and laying his hands on him he said, "Brother Saul, the Lord Jesus, who appeared to you on the road as you came, has sent me that you may receive your sight and be filled with the Holy Spirit." 18 Immediately there fell from his eyes [something] like scales, and he received his sight at once; and he arose and was baptized. (Acts 9:10-18, NKJV)

We get more details here, from Paul's testimony:

> **"Then a certain Ananias, a devout man according to the law, having a good testimony with all the Jews who dwelt [there], 13 came to me; and he stood and said to me, 'Brother Saul, receive your sight.' And at that same hour I looked up at him…" (Acts 22:12-13, NKJV)**

The actual healing came through his *faith*, by the laying on of hands and a command. Ananias understood his authority in Messiah.

In Matthew 17:21, Jesus said, "But this kind does not go out except by prayer and fasting." This text is not in all of the Greek manuscripts, so we don't know for sure if it was there originally. We do know that He at least said, "this kind can come out only by prayer" because of the record in Mark 9. And we know from other Scriptures, clearly, that fasting amplifies prayer. So personally, I figure that he did say it.

Jesus had already answered his disciples' question of "why couldn't we cast out the demon?" saying it was because of their unbelief. So the fasting and prayer would change *them*, not God. It would not change God's power or His willingness to help the boy. It would deal with the disciples' unbelief so that they could drive out the spirit.

All that being said, the prayer and fasting would be done beforehand, as Jesus apparently did here, as part of a lifestyle. The actual casting out of the demon was done with a word, by faith. He didn't ask the Father to do it for Him (Mt 17:18).

As far as I know there is *no* record in Scripture of asking God to bind or cast out a demon for us. He gave us the authority, in the Messiah, to do it. If we don't, he won't. He's given us jurisdiction. We can pray for a lot of things, but if there's something within our jurisdiction and responsibility to do, we'll get nowhere asking Him to do it.[2]

---

[2] I've seen exception to this with new, uneducated Christians, but eventually we're to grow into the recognition and exercise of our authority.

Imagine if your boss at work trained you, gave you a task, and then sent you to do it. He even gave you a badge so that others would know that you're authorized. You arrive on the scene and, instead of doing it, you go back to him and ask him to come out and do it for you. Would he do it?

What would make a person pray for God to heal the sick or cast out a demon when the Lord sent us saying, "Go, heal the sick…cast out demons, and lay hands on the sick and they'll recover"? Could it be that we don't believe He'll actually do it through us? But on the other hand, believing is what allows for the miracles.

Jesus' Legislature (His "Church") has been severely unaware of the authority we've been given in Him, by grace. The Scripture says that we are kings, in Him (e.g., Romans 5:17). The understanding of this was lost for centuries. I highly recommend Kenneth E. Hagin's book, "The Believer's Authority" (Legacy Edition, if possible).

I started studying healing and casting out demons 22 years ago. It's a vast subject that spans the Bible cover to cover. I've always loved the subject and seen its importance, but I was frustrated for years. I saw healings, deliverances, and miracles—some in my own body, some through me, some through others—but they were few and far between.

Then about four years ago I came to understand a few things that I was off about. These turned the light on, and I've seen an explosion of healing miracles ever since, wherever we go. I'm writing these truths for you now because they will result in more good if you use them.

I used to ask God (and sometimes plead with Him) to heal people. In the Old Testament, Abraham asked God to heal King Abimalech, and He did so (Genesis 20:7). Moses did similarly with Pharaoh. But Jesus didn't. We covered this above. His disciples/believers didn't either. When it came to evil spirits, I knew about the need to exercise the authority we have, in Messiah. But I still thought we should ask God to heal sicknesses. My misunderstanding came partly from two verses:

**Beloved, I wish above all things that thou mayest prosper and be in health, even as thy soul prospereth. (3John 2, KJV)**

John was addressing his good friend Gaius. His wish for him reveals the will of God for each of us, that we prosper in His will and plans for us, and that we be in health physically—in addition to prospering in soul through the Truth.

Here the King James Version translates this verse correctly. But most modern versions here translate "wish" as "pray"! This is not the standard, Greek word for pray. The word here is "wish" or "desire."

Prayer may be needed for revelation, for understanding, for God to send His Word in an area, for wisdom, for mercy, for intercession, etc. We pray, yes, and then we turn to the sick person and, by faith, do the works of Jesus.

The next passage is in James 5:

**Is anyone among you sick? Let him call for the elders of the church, and let them pray over him, anointing him with oil in the name of the Lord. (James 5:14, NKJV)**

The leaders here are called on to help. This takes faith and humility on the part of the sick person. They start with prayer, similar to the other examples listed earlier in this chapter. This is a powerful scene of united prayer. They pray by the Spirit whatever He gives them.

Then they anoint him with oil in the Name of the Lord. The oil, I see as a means to transfer power. God works through it similar to the laying on of hands (as in Mark 6:12).

**And the prayer [Literally: "vow"] of faith will save the sick [Literally: "weary"], and the Lord will raise him up. And if he has committed sins, he will be forgiven. (James 5:15, NKJV)**

Here is where there is a clear mistranslation. The word

"prayer" here means "vow." It does *not* mean prayer. Its other two uses in Scripture are Acts 18:18 and 21:23. This says the "vow of faith will save the weary, and the Lord will raise him up." It should never have been translated, "the prayer of faith will heal the sick." Next:

**Confess your trespasses to one another, and pray for one another, that you may be healed. (James 5:16, NKJV)**

I believe this, among other verses, reveals that sins can get between us and our healing (e.g., 1Cor 11:20-34, John 5:14). They can get between us and our *Healer*. At times we need to confess to each other sins we've committed against each other, and then to pray/intercede for each other—so that God's healing can reach us.

Notice that it says, "...that you may be healed." Though it may appear at first glance to be praying *for* healing—something we never see Jesus or His early disciples do in the rest of the whole New Testament—it is actually saying confess & pray, so nothing hinders you from being healed.

Things have changed completely and for the better for me.

A good friend of mine, who boldly preaches the Gospel around the world, was plagued by a series of terrible accidents. He severely damaged his back, went through several surgeries, and severely damaged his shoulder. He ended up on a hospital bed, in his living room, in a brace, in extreme pain.

I prayed and fasted for him. I went to visit him a couple times, laid hands on him and cried out to God. I prophesied accurately to him at one point, which encouraged him—but this was *the only way* I could help him at that time. I imagine he cried out to God for healing at that time too, but he wasn't miraculous healed this way.

A few months later, after discovering our authority and power to heal the sick, my wife and I paid him another visit. He had recovered some, but he could only raise his left arm about 15 degrees from his side. Also his nerves on his toes had died, resulting in extreme pain—his brain would send a signal down to his toes and when it could not get a normal response it would send excruciating pain signals back every few minutes.

This brother's wife also had knee pain, and she had just been crying out to God for help and considering going to a doctor. (I believe God heard that prayer and sent us to help). My wife commanded her knee to heal, and it did so immediately. No prayer was made other than possibly a quick prayer of thanksgiving or acknowledgment. God healed her, through my wife's faith and command.

Then, through simply using what I've been teaching you about here, the brother was healed that night. His toe pain stopped immediately, and after laying hands on him twice briefly, he could raise his arm high like the other one.

We had learned to use our authority. We had learned we've been empowered, just as the Scripture has been saying all along.

In Luke 9, thousands of people had come to hear and be healed by Jesus, but they had no food. Jesus told his disciples, "You give them something to eat"—with only five loaves and two fish (Lk 9:13). And He gave the food to His disciples to feed the people. Isn't it wonderful how he loves to *include us* in His work? Now what if they were unwilling? What if they said to him, "No, Teacher, we can't do this."? Would the Teacher have been happy? But they went and did it; they believed Him and took action, and he was pleased, and the miracle was done.

Then in Luke 10, Jesus sent them out and said, "In whatever city you enter, and they receive you…heal the sick and say to them, The Kingdom of God has come near you" (Luke 10:9-10). Could they do it? Did they?

Prayer is extremely important and should fill our lives. But the things that God tells *us* to do in His name, we should do, rather than turning back to Him and asking Him to do them.

# Chapter 7
# The Mind of Christ

Scripture says, "we have the mind of Christ" (1Cor 2:16). Because we're His Body we have access to it, but we have to exchange our own thinking for His holy thinking to utilize it. Our thinking compared to the world's should become like a butterfly compared to an earthworm. The first thing Jesus proclaimed was "Change your thinking[3] for the Kingdom of God is near." This is an obligation for all of us. "Change your thinking and believe the Gospel" (Mark 1:15).

Seven times the New Testament states that "All things are possible" or "Nothing is impossible"—with God and to the one who believes (Mt 17:20, 19:26; Mk 9:23, 10:27, 14:36; Lk 1:37, 18:27). This is part of the mind of the Messiah.

Scripture also says,

"Is anything too hard for the LORD? At the appointed time I will return to you, according to the time of life, and Sarah shall have a son." (Genesis 18:14, NKJV)

'Ah, Lord GOD! Behold, You have made the heavens and the earth by Your great power and outstretched arm. There is nothing too hard for You. (Jeremiah 32:17, NKJV)

"Behold, I [am] the LORD, the God of all flesh. Is there anything too hard for Me? (Jeremiah 32:27, NKVJ)

We need to line our thinking up with this, exchanging any lower thinking of ours with it.

Faith sees through the Words of God, "God *wants to* heal

---
[3] Literal, English meaning of "repent."

me," "God *can* heal me," and as we get the Word pumping through our veins, "God *will heal* me."

The Word of God brings faith, when allowed into our hearts, and faith brings God's miraculous power and provision into the various areas of our lives. We should always bow our heads, step aside and make way for the entrance of God's Words.

**...receive with meekness the implanted word.... (James 1:21, NJKV)**

**The entrance of Your words gives light; It gives understanding to the simple. (Psalm 119:130, NKJV)**

**"But to this one I will look, to him who is humble and contrite of spirit, and who trembles at My word. (Isaiah 66:2, NASB)**

Utilizing the mind of the Messiah will bring more healing into our lives. I was doing outreach in a mall with a group one day. I saw a woman limping, and I asked if she would like help. I was doing like Jesus, who said, "Do you want to be well?" She pretended to not speak English. But her daughter with her also needed healing. After she received it, her mother said, "OK."

I checked her leg length, and clearly one was shorter than the other. As I commanded it go grow out, in the Name of Jesus, it did, and she was healed. Another woman saw that and smiled. I called her over. She had had three surgeries on her left arm for RSD, and extreme pain in it. I commanded it to heal and God healed it instantly.

At that point those of us doing the outreach were all together in the same area, and several miracles started breaking out. One brother on the team came and asked if I'd check his legs too in case they were uneven. It turned out that they were. Using the same faith and expectation, I commanded the short one to grow out, and it didn't move. I persisted, using faith, but there was no change.

Then I utilized the mind of Christ. I knew that He wants to use all of His Body, and I remembered that there was someone on the team that hadn't healed the sick yet. I called him over. He commanded the leg once, and it immediately grew out to match the other.

Thinking and believing like God in this area also requires knowing the will of God about healing. We know it by faith also; it's revealed through His Word. In Africa, when teaching this material, I skipped the section on the will of God concerning healing. They didn't need to hear it.

But the Western world, having the Scriptures readily available, has been attacked for centuries by the enemy in this area. He's worked hard to keep people from believing God wants to heal all, because healing is the heavenly, explosive, mass-marketing tool for evangelism. It's what brought the huge crowds to Jesus.

If we don't believe God even wants to heal, we will always doubt whether he will heal. Knowing that He wants to heal is part of lining up with the will of God and having the mind of Messiah.

Many, many teachers sent from God have written on the subject of God's will concerning healing. If there is any doubt in your mind, or if you'd like to strengthen your understanding and assurance in this area, I suggest you go through the recommended material listed at the end of this book.

When the disciples faced a demon-sickness that they couldn't seem to heal, they did not create a doctrine that God doesn't want to heal that type of problem. They didn't make their results the standard. Instead, they went to Jesus, as children, and asked, "Why couldn't we cast it out?"

Jesus healed the boy, revealing that even though the disciples couldn't cast it out at their present state of learning, they would be able to do so eventually.

I've asked the Teacher the same question a couple times, and the answers I received resulted in more learning for me and more healing and freedom for others.

# Chapter 8
# At Times, Find the Cause

**And behold, there was a woman who had a spirit of infirmity eighteen years, and was bent over and could in no way raise herself up. (Luke 13:11, NKJV)**

A friend and I were in a public place and asked a woman if she had any pains or sicknesses that she needed help with. She told us about her foot pain, and I pointed at it and commanded it to heal. We had her walk across the room and back, and then she told us, "When I was walking away, I felt it getting better and then walking back toward you, it started getting worse." She had a spirit of infirmity.

So we commanded the spirit to go, and she was totally healed. She asked, "How did you do that?" We said, "Jesus."

Sometimes we'll get "discerning of spirits" (1Cor 12:10) to let us know a spirit is involved. Other times we just know by observation.

While teaching a class on this subject, I had a student command a woman's back pain to go. At first there was no change, but the second time he did so she felt the pain moving. I said, "It's a spirit." He then commanded the pain to go again, and I told him, "Now that we know it's a spirit, specifically command the spirit to go." Then he did so, and she was freed/healed.

Sometimes the cause is ignorance on our part. For example, my wife and I got a man healed who had been in a motorcycle accident. Immediately his leg pain left him, and he could walk better. He came to where I was teaching the next couple days and kept asking for more help. Though he could walk unassisted now, something wasn't fixed. Through translation, we eventually found out it was *numbness* that he was asking about. I hadn't been commanding numbness to go! So I did, and it was then healed instantly.

A few weeks ago, a friend of mine commanded a man's arm to work in Jesus' Name, and it got a little mobility. Then he found out he'd had a stroke, so he laid his hands on his brain and commanded *it* to work properly, and immediately the man could use that arm well. He excitedly started shadow boxing with both arms!

Sometimes we can only go so far with people, according to the permission they give us. I saw a man sweeping a parking garage one night as I got off work. I asked him if he needed any healing, and he humbly said, "Yes. My ankle." I laid my hand on it and commanded it to heal. It noticeably got better, but not fully. So I started to use faith again, but when he heard the name, "Jesus" he pulled his foot away. He was rejecting the Healer, and he didn't get any more healing that night, though I tried.

You'll also see people who'd rather keep their sicknesses than get healed by the risen King Jesus, because they don't want to have to believe in Him. If they reject you, you can lovingly say to them, "Nevertheless, the Kingdom of God has come near you" (Luke 10:11).

But if people give us room, including unbelievers, we should persist. A friend of mine asked an atheist man if he had any sickness or pain. The man challenged him defiantly to heal his headache and back. My friend commanded them to heal, and they didn't the first time. So he did again. On the second or third time the man was totally healed. Not only that, he had a tumor on his stomach that he hadn't told anyone about. When God healed him of those other things, the tumor disappeared too. The man became a disciple of Jesus. We immersed him in a river shortly after that, and he was filled with the Spirit and started walking with Jesus.

When bringing God's healing to people, as in everything, the Holy Spirit is our Helper. We go; we use our faith; we are to be doers of the Word—and He'll help gloriously from time to time.

At a restaurant, I asked a woman if she had any sickness or

pains, and she answered self-defensively, "Why?!" I told her that we are Christians and that Jesus heals people through us. She then let me know that the left atrium of her heart was enlarged. I commanded it to heal, and it obeyed. Immediately the pain left, and she could swing her arm around, when before she couldn't lift it all the way up.

There is so much more I'd love to share with you on this whole topic, but this is it for now. 'Peace and all blessings *through* you, in Jesus' Name, to those He died to save and heal.

# Recommended Resources

With all of these resources, always test all things by the Scripture. Always listen to The Teacher (Ecc 12:11). And please, never divide or cause division based on teachers (1Cor 3:4-5,21-22, 4:5-6).

### Authority to Heal & Free People:
- The Believer's Authority, by Kenneth E. Hagin (Book, video messages available)
- Speak to the Mountain, by Andrew Wommack (Audio message)

### The Will of God Regarding Healing:
- Biblical Healing, by TL Osborn (Book, audio book)
- Healing the Sick, by TL Osborn (Book, audio book)
- Andrew Wommack material on the subject
- Kenneth E. Hagin material on the subject
- John G. Lake material on the subject
- Derek Prince material on the subject

### Building Further on the Foundation:
- Charles Ndifon

### More from David O'Brien (see website below):
- Return to Acts Christianity (Book, Audio messages)
- Jesus The King (Evangelistic Booklet)

## ActsChristianity.org